# Steven Spielberg
## He Makes Great Movies

by Marcia L. McAllister

illustrated by Luciano Lazzarino

Rourke Enterprises  Vero Beach, Florida

Manufactured in the United States of America

## Library of Congress Cataloging-in-Publication Data

McAllister, Marcia L., 1940-
Steven Spielberg, he makes great movies / Marcia L.
McAllister.
    p.   cm. —(Reaching your goal)
    Summary: Discusses how Steven Spielberg obtained his
goal of becoming a movie director. Includes advice on
setting and reaching goals.
    1. Spielberg, Steven, 1947-     —Juvenile literature.
2. Motion picture producers and directors—United States—
Biography—Juvenile literature. [1. Spielberg, Steven,
1947-  .  2. Motion picture producers and directors.]
I. Title.   II. Series.
PN1998.3.S65M34   1989
791.43'0233'0924—dc19
[B]                                                88-15794
[92]                                                    CIP
ISBN 0-86592-427-9                                      AC

The actors are ready to act. The camera people are ready to film. "Action!" shouts a man. The actors begin acting. The camera people roll the cameras. A movie is being made. The man shouting "action" is Steven Spielberg. He is a famous movie director. Steven Spielberg makes great movies.

One of the movies that Steven Spielberg made is *Jaws*. *Jaws* is about a huge shark that frightens people. Steven read the book *Jaws* first. He thought it would make a good movie. He was right. The movie was a big hit. More people went to see *Jaws* than had gone to see any other movie.

Another movie Steven Spielberg made is *E.T.: The Extra-Terrestrial*. It is about a creature from outer space named E.T. In the movie, E.T.'s spaceship takes off in a hurry. E.T. is left behind on Earth. He is all alone. But E.T. meets an Earth boy named Elliot. Elliot is lonely. E.T. and Elliot become best friends. They have exciting adventures together.

The lonely boy in the movie *E. T.* was much like Steven Spielberg. When Steven was a boy, he was lonely too. His family moved many times because of his father's work. Moving so much made it hard for Steven to make many friends.

As a youngster, Steven spent hours of time alone in his room. It was always a big mess. Everyone stayed out of Steven's room. It was his private place for playing and thinking. And Steven was always thinking. What did Steven think about? He thought about how to play scary jokes on his sisters!

Once Steven really scared his sisters. He put a light inside a plastic skull. Steven put a cap on the skull and hung it in a closet.

Steven told his sisters that there was something in the closet. As they opened the closet door, Steven turned on the light. The skull glowed in the dark. Steven's sisters screamed. Steven laughed. Then his sisters laughed too.

The frightening jokes Steven played on his sisters may have given him ideas for the scary movies he makes. One scary movie is called *Poltergeist.* In that movie, ghosts haunt a house. The ghosts do many bad things to frighten the people who live in the house.

Was Steven Spielberg always a famous movie director? No, but he began directing movies when he was **very** young. Steven's father often filmed the family on their camping trips. Steven always told his father how and what to film. One day, Mr. Spielberg handed the camera to his son. "You do the filming," he said. Steven did. He soon learned how to work the camera very well.

Steven enjoyed filming very much. He saved his money and bought his own movie camera. He was twelve years old at the time.

Steven put his new camera to good use. He joined a Boy Scout photography class. He used his camera to make a movie for the class. The movie was only three minutes long. It was about a stagecoach robbery. Steven had fun making the movie. He earned a merit badge for making the movie.

After making the movie for his Boy Scout class, Steven set a goal for himself. He wanted to become a movie director. Steven worked hard. He practiced filming all kinds of things. Steven liked filming his family. "Mom," Steven said one day, "don't start cooking until I get my camera!"

Steven set up special things to film. He used model trains to film train crashes. First Steven studied the trains crashing from different angles. Then he decided how to film the crash. Steven filmed the crashes over and over until they were just right.

When Steven was sixteen, he made his first long movie. It was a science fiction movie called *Firelight*. Steven wrote the story. He talked some of his friends into acting the parts. He directed the movie and filmed the action.

*Firelight* was shown in a movie theater. Steven talked to a theater owner near his home. The theater owner agreed to show the movie for one night. Steven sold tickets. He sold enough tickets to pay for making the movie. Steven even had a little money left over for himself.

Shortly after Steven made *Firelight*, his family moved. They moved to Los Angeles, California. That's where many movies are made in big movie studios.

Steven went to the movie studios often. He watched movies being made. He asked lots of questions. Steven wanted to learn all he could about making movies. He wanted very much to reach his goal of becoming a famous movie director.

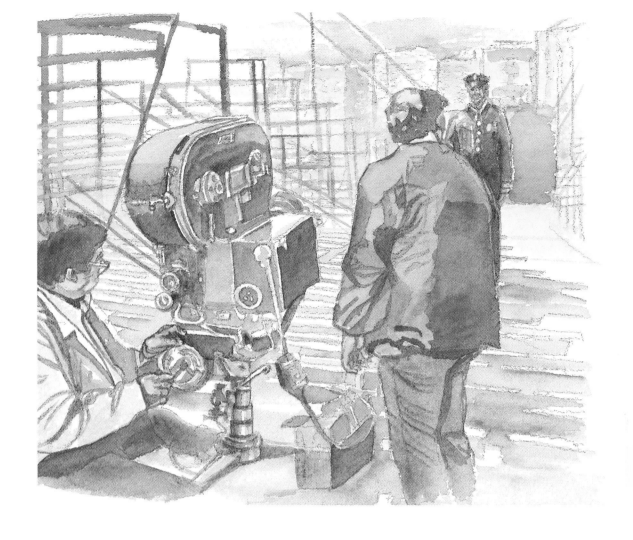

In college, Steven learned more about making movies. Steven and a friend at school made a movie together. The bosses at a big movie studio saw the movie. They liked it. They gave Steven a job. The job was to direct TV shows. After directing TV shows for many years, Steven began directing movies.

While Steven was busy directing movies, he met and married an actress. Her name is Amy Irving. Steven and Amy have a son. His name is Max.

Steven has been making movies a long time. He still works hard. But Steven always takes time off from his busy day to play with Max.

Steven Spielberg has met his goal. He is now a well-known movie director. People like Steven's movies. Some people go to see them over and over again.

Today, Steven Spielberg helps other people to meet their goals. Steven has his own movie company. He gives young movie directors a chance to make movies. He helps these men and women to do their best.

# Reaching Your Goal

What are your goals? Here are some steps to help you reach them.

1. **Decide on your goal.**
   It may be a short-term goal like one of these:
   learning to ride a bike
   getting a good grade on a test
   keeping your room clean
   It may be a long-term goal like one of these:
   learning to read
   learning to play the piano
   becoming a lawyer

2. **Decide if your goal is something you really can do.**
   Do you have the talent you need?
   How can you find out? By trying!
   Will you need special equipment?
   Perhaps you need a piano or ice skates.
   How can you get what you need?
   Ask your teacher or your parents.

**3. Decide on the first thing you must do.**
Perhaps this will be to take lessons.

**4. Decide on the second thing you must do.**
Perhaps this will be to practice every day.

**5. Start right away.**
Stick to your plan until you reach your goal.

**6. Keep telling yourself, "I can do it!"**

Good Luck! Maybe some day you will become a movie director like Steven Spielberg!

# Reaching Your Goal Books

**Beverly Cleary** She Makes Reading Fun

**Bill Cosby** Superstar

**Jesse Jackson** A Rainbow Leader

**Ted Kennedy, Jr.** A Lifetime of Challenges

**Christa McAuliffe** Reaching for the Stars

**Dale Murphy** Baseball's Gentle Giant

**Dr. Seuss** We Love You

**Samantha Smith** Young Ambassador

**Michael Jordan** A Team Player

**Steven Spielberg** He Makes Great Movies

**Charles Schulz** Great Cartoonist

**Cher** Singer and Actress

**Ray Kroc** McDonald's Man

**Hans Christian Andersen** A Fairy Tale Life

**Henry Cisneros** A Hard Working Mayor

**Jim Henson** Creator of the Muppets

Rourke Enterprises, Inc.
P.O. Box 3328
Vero Beach, FL 32964